OTHER BOOKS BY JARED SMITH:

A Sphere Encased in Fires and Life (NYQ Books)
That's How It Is (Stubborn Mule Press)
Shadows Within The Roaring Fork (FlowStone Press)
This Town (co-authored with Kyle Laws, Liquid Light Press)
To The Dark Angels (NYQ Books)
The Collected Poems: 1971-2011 (NYQ Books)
Grassroots (Wind Publications)
Looking Into The Machinery (Tamarack Editions)
The Graves Grow Bigger Between Generations (Higganum
Hill Books)
Where Images Become Imbued With Time (Puddin'head Press)
Lake Michigan and Other Poems (Puddin'head Press)
Walking the Perimeters of the Plate Glass Window Factory
(BirchBrook Press)
Keeping the Outlaw Alive (Erie Street Press)
Dark Wing (Charred Norton Press)
Song of the Blood (The Smith Press)

The Shoebox at the
End of the Universe

Poems by Jared Smith

STUBBORN MULE PRESS
DEVIL'S ELBOW, MO

Stubborn Mule Press

Devil's Elbow, Missouri

Copyright © Jared Smith, 2024

First edition 1 3 5 7 9 10 8 6 4 2

ISBN: 978-1-958182-51-2

LCCN: 2023952035

Author photo: Russell J.W. Smith

Cover and title page image: Jon Lee Grafton

Acknowledgments:

The author expresses his thanks to the following publications in which some of the poems in this volume first appeared:

Bristlecone published "Watching a Downy Woodpecker," and "Within the Shadows of Invisible"

Chiron Review published "The Ghosts we Carry," "Just Another Sunday," and "The Shoebox at the end of the Universe"

Fixed and Free Anthology published "Among the Words"

Home Planet News: published "The Secret," "The Earth is More Immense," and "Finding Yourself"

The Pedestal Magazine: published "Before the Storm"

The Somerville Times: published "Call it a Train."

Turtle Island Quarterly published "A Deep Wilderness," "The Everywhere," "The Before Light of Morning," and "Only an Infinite Moment in Time"

TABLE OF CONTENTS

Dedicated to:

Deb Smith

…His eyes shine like those amber-lensed lanterns
railway men used to hang on the caboose, or the
revelations poets used to hang at the end of a
train of thought.

-Joseph Hutchison

The Messenger-Sprit
in human flesh
is assigned a dependable,
self-reliant, versatile,
thoroughly poet existence
upon its sojourn in life

-Gregory Corso

Learning About Poetry

In evening a tired farm hand kneels
down on the bank of a slow rolling river
near a stretch of wild grain rice.
In his hand is a lined pad of paper,
and each sheet has words written on it.
He tears off the top one and makes a canoe of it,
folding it deftly in his calloused hands.
He sets it on the river and lights a match,
setting fire to the folds of its bow.
Then releases it.
It sails its light into the river.
The river hisses and it is gone.
It does not go very far at all.
He crafts and lights another one,
and another, and one by one sends each one
waiting to see if one will catch the wind.

Call it a Train

Let's say a train is rushing toward you and
the engineer is drinking a bottle of Red Ball whiskey.
You are not aware of it because the tracks curve
over the horizon where autumn leaves are golden
and the rails themselves are so hard and inscrutable.
It's a long way off and you are holding a butterfly
perched on your hand just lightly fluttering its wings.
There is no way off the track. It is over a steep gorge.

You have built your dream house on this railway track.
Monks climb up and down its wallboards each evening.
They fly their kites out your windows at daybreak.
Their feet are the sounds of heartbeats on your soul.
You are expecting some sort of life-changing surprise
and have learned to fold origami cranes from napkins.
You idly hope they can hoist the weights that you
require.

Among the Words

I have lived so long among words
they are become my familiars almost,
pressing their warm fur to my throat
or nestling deep around my groin.
I have come to know them well,
their secrets, their scent, their taste,
the spaces between letters and sounds,
the spaces between vision and letters.

This is perhaps what it is to be a poet
who has grown old among the mountains,
who has fought against popular wars,
who has won awards for words written,
who has thought your beauty was a symphony,
who has listened to the music of time
at a place where it separates from words.

The Secret

The secret slickers like silver
needle thin in loam beneath the forest floor,
happens at the corners of your eyes,
burbles from the throats of morning finches
dancing from limb to limb along each bough,
waits silently where people do not speak
snapping suddenly awake to strangle them
when their days are darkest and erupt in light.

The Earth is More Immense

Wide open flaming mouth of dragon,
rising feathered wing of phoenix,
fly into the flames of your nightmares
and expand there, for we can only change
when what has encased us perishes…

and so a madness spreads through the mind
of a landscape too worn down by industry,
disease, money-making, and the viruses
of animals penned too long in tract homes.
The earth itself seethes, and rivers run dry,
hardened mud cracks where plants grew
and fires begin to roar from man's creations,
the cigarettes, campfires, bullets, ignorance,
 and more than can be contained any longer flame
from sheltered canyons, the dried dead trees
flaring suddenly upward and laying their smoke
and ash across a countryside grown hot
as the iron of its machinery driven lust.

It is a hot, hard grind, and homes are lost
and lives are lost, and each year the cost is greater.
A civilization cannot contemplate its coming end
when its leaders' lungs are filled with the ash
that remains from its dreams and odysseys.
They cannot plan when their lungs are filled with death.
I have seen it all, from the faintest flicker of grass fires
to the cascading walls of flame surrounding mountain
towns cut off from the highways that were their birth
to the raging ovens of flames that come for all...
the deer, the moose, the squirrels, the mountain lions,
all that is innocent, and man in his ignorance.

The earth is more immense in its little part of the cosmos
than all the bombs we have dropped in all our wars.
And there are rules of physics and matter and mortality
that are understood by water and rock and mass
and absence itself in the mystery of space that are not
in the understanding of the imperfections we call life.

Before the Storm

Two days out before the storm
we began gathering candles
from all those places one hides them,
puts them away for when needed,
old ones limned with the scent of mothballs,
half melted Christmas candles,
whatever we could find and matches,
a bic lighter, an old iron lantern,

and yet wind blew the darkness in.
The human body is a fragile frame
for all the fires you carry within you.
Winter carves us out, bares our ribs
each cycle of twelve new moons.
Some leaves tossed upon the wind
last longer than others but dust is dust.

The human body is an invincible tunnel
running between darkness and lightning
beneath all the generations of moons
ever written of…

and what the Data Measures,

is not what makes a person
marry or build a home or work a job
or overthrow a government or tyrant
or lie down in the sweet grass of a meadow
filling his day only with the thrum of insects

gathering pollen and spreading seeds
in chaotic patterns across the universe;

What the data measures is
merely the size and shape of temporary
tubes of matter that meander like rivers
descended like snow fallen on mountains,
descending to the valleys below matched
to the contour of land rather than spirit.

A Deep Wilderness

I walk along a path that shadow animals have made
from one hunting ground to another across stone,
and I reach down to pluck the only sign of life
that is obvious in this harsh setting...a seed
where nothing has yet set down its roots.
I press it to my lips and bite hard into its skin.

Folded inside this hard shell of a seed is a wilderness
seething to escape, but still shielded from the winds
that will brush and whisper among its leaves
and from those leaves lift a song
that carries an army of tumbled branches,
roots reaching out, grasping earth and holding.
All these lives from one seed, wind-pollinated.

The tree will not grow on barren rock.
The leaves lie dormant without rain.
The seed a time capsule cemented in sunlight.

There is a word for this
but it is beyond the range of what is known.
Is it that a word is a seed as well in a wind
that waits for other seeds before it blooms,

sending out an angry army of conflicting thought,
tumbled branches and roots, singing first in monotone?
What would you lay down in print to make meaning
of scattered leaves becoming maple, pine, aspen, oak
tossed by winds they do not have an understanding of?

It is that time of year the sap is rising
and old men have placed tin buckets along dark trunks
watching and waiting to see what secrets drop in,
boiling it all down and hoping for something darker,
sweeter that will melt in the mouth, on the tongue,
and whatever it is they will give it word, a seed
with meaning that will stretch across generations.

In the beginning that is what it was.
If there is one seed then there will be more
and unknown conversations will take place.
From the forest floor detritus fresh soil will appear
and who knows what invasive species will hold
or what breaks down the stone of meanings.
What brings what life to what dark seeds,
whether fire or frost or rain or drought?
In the beginning this is what it was.

.

Shadows follow shadows that we believe in
but the world and word are what they are.

Together in Our Age

The storm still grows in intensity.
We had seen it coming, the dark clouds
the wind screaming across mountains
the bar charts and weathermen on t.v.
We had seen the crops fail in drought,
watched the western mountains burn
as the unbearable heat came upon us
and our lungs filled with ashen forests.

The tremor in my hands cannot hold
any longer the beliefs I have abided by.
They fail, but together we move forward
still even though the windows rattle
and the wind roars in ways we knew not.
I try to keep you warm against my side,
try to set this new house against the storm.
We had seen it coming for years, the dark clouds,
the destruction and desolation of our time on earth.
I have tried to keep you warm. I try
with all my heart and words of experience
though the books in my library grow musty
and the bottles of ideas I have drunk grow stale
I have nothing without you and never have.

We are together in a new century
where ideas seem smaller within a larger audience.
We move into a smaller house and tell each other
it is spacious. The storm peels siding from our exterior,
and we are emptier than we would wish or seem,
a man and woman in a home in America.

*

Deer come in the morning
when shadows melt into the darkness
before I have my coffee cup in hand,
deer soft as the grasses they graze upon,
gentle caresses I would hold to my breast
as soft as velvet, warm as their eyes,
I would hold them if I could and they
are not afraid but stay their distance
and stay within the shadings of dawn.
In the daylight they are gone, and
I do not see them until driving into
my driveway at night their eyes red,
demonic and then backing away again
into the grasses that surround us.

*

We drive down to the Patapsco River Valley,
park under an old railroad overpass and enter
a time of vanished industrialization, old estates
not unlike our own and walk among the stones
and along the old rail embankments along the
free-flowing crystal clear waters for miles where
the dams have been torn away and water flows
to the sea and migratory fish begin to spawn again.
We have come to this place which is old and used
and find that it is replenished with what we wish.
There is peace in this. The storm is what it is.

Transient Things

I have packed my memories in transient things.
A mink crossing the hand-hewn bridge below my
    cabin.
A blonde girl knocking on my fire escape window in
    New York.
Abandoned decaying piers along the Hudson,
the fish so cold they are wet socks when you pull
    them up.

What begins as a trickle of water in a high mountain
    meadow
becomes a stream shining the sun from its surface
    rushing
to the valleys below, becomes a shining song of life
dipping into the heavy muddy roll of centuries. And
    homes

lived in long enough to gather a few dustpans of my
    skin and
uniquely varied landscapes to imprint their elements
    into my bones.

These bones will collect themselves and the dust
    that covered them
in time when our globe devours itself in fire. They
    will be
what they have become from experience
    remembered unplanned.

These are transient things, drafty houses where my
    shadows
cross with the shadows of other strap-holders,
    renters, tenants. Scarecrows in Kansas wear the
    ragged clothes of men like me.

The Ghosts We Carry

I am fascinated by the ghosts shrouding your shoulders.
In sunlight they are transparent as your thoughts,
their dance clothes and prize possessions long gone,
their skin too, only the brittle bone of their fingers
as shadows holding on to their homes and memories.
I don't imagine you are aware of their lips nibbling
at your ear lobes, brushing as mist across your hair.

In this candle-lit room where liquor flows freely
they too flow freely, their words the words of family
dust cloths left on bannisters, bad omens of lay-offs
that happened just before babies were born, and of
fires that swept across the open fields before harvest.
Awful memories overlaid with births and jewelry
and the rain-fresh spring scent of lilacs in bloom,
the poisonous lily-of-the-valley seducing senses
with an aroma so complex and urgently gentle,
I am fascinated by the weave of the presence knitting
our lips together in this moment and by their words
somehow surviving the bodies that bore them
and shrouding our futures together as one.

Somewhere Around Three Each Afternoon

The guys gather at the donut shop.
Painful years with good intents
gathered in their worn work clothes,
they are slouched on cane backed chairs
and there is a mustiness about them.
Their words are the deep rumble
of well-oiled, hard used antique machinery,
it's gears worn down and starting to slip
but still humming along, familiar as time.

Their hands hold the memories of how
to mine ore from the earth and melt it down
or sow seeds that will feed a nation
or replace the turbines within a dam,
between them murmuring one to another
about the last time anyone called them in

The Old Man Did Not Die Today

The old man did not die today though
the doctors said his kidneys failed four months ago.
A law of physics was broken as he strolled the lakeshore
at the hour green grass rose up to greet gray shadows
He walked the paths of constellations across twilight and
there was something in his heart that kept him going.
Birds filled the shadows that surrounded him with song.
He did not know what he was doing or where going
but was at peace and therefore found his way home.

Self-Portrait

The rawness of his face
was the rawness of the grasses
that grew beyond his cabin,
his eyes torn by watching earth
too closely, the turn of seasons
amplified by distance to the sun
and the cacophony of continents
held upon an ocean of iron magma.

The Everywhere

I have been the wind
      have ascended the stairs
            danced as water on a silver stream
I have shaken the house
      worn the robes of ancient gods
            lived long in the light of evening
                and learned to sing from shadows
Ohhh these are gone in the mist of time

When you enter the awareness
      you touch all things simultaneously
            there are no words for going back
When you enter there is no direction
      the stars are in your blood
            the miles of space that were separation
When you leave you cannot come back
      but what you left comes back into you.

You enter the everywhere.

Not Much and Nothing

Not much has changed here.
The grasses have grown higher
and the flowers royal blues and purples
so thick one's feet get tangled in them.
The days grow longer in their shadows
And winds glow dust across the windows.
Not much has changed.

Nothing happens in death.
The insignificant bacteria and viruses
may tear at the fabric of a universe
and flesh may swell then fall away,
but those things are not in death.
They are merely of the wind.

In the Before Light of Morning

In the before light of morning
when water still condenses from thin air
as do shadows that might be animals
forged from the darkness about them and
everything you have dreamed of is still
waiting to take shape in our world
where people have learned to fly
and communicate with the dead
generations that dreamed of us
and wrote epic poems and journeys
that would be melted down from rock,
words that would be carried on ether
condensing in minds before sun rises.

In the before light of morning
all energy comes from the sun but
energy is only the transfer, the flow,
from ungodly heat to ungodly cold,
from lightness to darkness. Without
darkness the before light is nothing.
An ashen figure dropping icicles to the wind
which exists only in a tomb of the mind.

In the before light of morning
grande dames rise on wings of lavender lace,
owls return to their haunted trees
and herons stand silent in the mist,
one foot firm in the mud and one in feather.

These are caverns you cannot rise from.
Their gray walls are ethereal and ghostly
filled with the shadows of spirits
landscaped in the guttural world of oink.

Just Another Sunday

Sundays are rock candy mountains
where all the honest hardworking children of God
have their blood pressure rise up in the sweetness
of one more day with the family before Monday's

ragged catastrophe of lost appointments
miscarriages of justice, misaddressed Wanted posters,
and stolen identities, the dustbowl of our generation
wound up in a paycheck with Covid greeting card
posted via FB and hacked by Russian agents.

Autumn in the Crucible

The living is a spirit of order
           an arrow opposed to time
           a beetle on an exposed slab
                       the slab disorder and winning
surrounded by halos in a dusty coffee house
words clinking of glasses rebellion and love
           an arrow opposed to time

And the leaves always rearrange themselves
when they fall in the failing light of autumn.

This Day in the Year of the Crucible

A man seeking civilization
in the barren fields of his own time,

I am an albatross
eyes gone gray against the mist
wave tossed fickle feathered
and hung from a bastard's beard.

There is no calmness in what we are.
Waves storm against the shore
thousands of miles from here
and continents break their backs.

I have come from this, flown
from the darkness between my legs
one ragged sailing ship to another
maggots eating out my brain.

I am appalled and afraid of
what is in me and upon me,
my memories clouded by sea
and lands I cannot land on.

Finding Yourself

You are standing on the bedrock peak
overlooking a valley below Spencer Mountain
and a warm dry July evening wraps about you,
shelters your shoulders from the upkeep you meant
to do, and the pine trees and aspens sing in their
shadows with the wind that speaks of the high
country. Their song mixes with that of the last
hummingbirds and the blood pumping through
your heart, and the chirp of fox squirrel headed
     to ground.

The valley is disappearing below you,
and you wait until the distant lights of towns
are replaced over time by the stars above.
It has taken years to arrive at this place
although from the beginning you never left.
And really does it matter? You breathe deeply
and the world goes on, the wind, the music,
the time it takes to find yourself in this wilderness.

At Three in the Morning

I don't count the ones whose names I didn't know.
There are clouds on the horizon or what I see of it
stretched between these stained brick buildings.
I'll be thinking of all of them again this evening.
I do not owe them anything. They are my life.

Each one of them has a grizzled meaning.
Mice and rats gather around their grunting.
Crickets are attracted by their smell.
There is a place for all things great and small.

Each subway car contains rows of cows
bemused by the speed of city lights.
I think that I have known some of them,
singled them out but, it is hard to say.
Perhaps they merely wore similar clothes,
perhaps they clutched their secrets empty
of anything that mattered in the course of things.

Still there are too many rattling keys outside and
I don't like them to visit at three in the morning,

Outside Minetta Tavern, Greenwich Village

Everything in the city is stacked.
The money the apartments, the deals
          one layer over the other,
I tell the girl I am leading around
the pipes, the gutters, the sewers,
the subways, all hollow tubes and tunnels
beneath Minetta Tavern and the law school
abutting on Washington Square alongside
the watchmakers playing chess among
professors and pretenders and the young.

Put your hand in, you find time itself is a river
          and flows over the pipes
that have been laid down like picked bones and
hidden below the gutters of another generation.
And the men and the women are but mostly meat
          strutting beside the gutters
where when their soles tire and fall they are
licked softly clean by the river flowing through,
and life picks them up and goes its way.

And everything is stacked.
The concrete sandwich roof of our city
          rising high one generation

above the next, concrete boxes, cubicles
for life and loving where lights are strung on wires
in evening as stars would be if there were stars to see.

Above them all this evening, each layer, lie
the mammatus clouds of infinity, and beneath
these stand the grandest houses of densest stone,
because where the most gracious lives have ended
in broken dreams or encased in paste and diamonds
the houses are thickest and heaviest and darkest
where the buried rivers flow sweet water
beneath tarmac and sweat and stone
        again stone
where the tunnels of creativity have been cut
by those who have lived in those tombs before.
Still, we have the green shoots of wildflowers
forcing their way upward through the cracks.

They have their own trade I say, their way,
taking in all the glorious wreaths they lay out,
the candlelit restaurants and shadowed rooms
where lovers give all they have to give, and

music floats from the fingers of the shadows.
And music too is time tumbling over the rocky
shores of the river we share beneath the stars.

Only an Infinite Moment in Time

By lunchtime I have set many deals on paper.
I am alive with all the dollars I have moved
and scared by the lies I have gotten away with.
I sweep a hand across my face and put away the cell.
Turn it off. Walk out among the other gray coats,
twisting between the laughter of young girls and
the sweaty bravado of hard hot men on the prowl.
The sun is blazing upon the concrete sidewalks
and the lights confused between red and green.
In New York you never stop walking at the end
of one block or street crossing, you just turn
corners and keep putting one foot before the other.

I've never been inside St. Peter's before but today
the door is closed but unlatched as I guess it always is.
I am ashamed that I have never been here in the quiet.
A ghost sits in the third pew from the front listening
to candles flickering in glass tubes on the wall.
Perhaps those flames are prayers or the ghost a shadow.
I have not been here long enough to know and
        never will.

The ceiling is the ceiling, as high as believers can build,
and the holy icons of gold are stars in its firmament.
I am at peace, and somehow god in a box is peaceful.
I wonder at how a god that sees and is all things is
best seen within a box, a frame that closes upon itself,
while here I am but the son of man and I am the
Eucharist.

In the Waiting Room of the Ophthalmologist

There are not many poems about ophthalmologist
offices but I've been sitting here and I'm a poet and
I look at the tan carpet and the white walls and the
hardback chairs where simple hard-working people
sit simply waiting like me all in their scrubbed best
looking selves like they'd like to be since after all it's
important the doctor knows how capable they are
and that they're important and should be cared for
carefully having showered this morning and put on
the clothes they choose to put their best feet forward
leaning on the partners who drove
        them here,
so that the insouciant blonde is wearing faded jeans
torn at the knees and the woman with bags under
her eyes has her hubby leaning
        bored against her shoulder
and the two ladies held up by strollers are dressed in
white soft silk and the fat lady with a cane is wearing
leopard spotted skin tights with the finest silk floral
pattern blouse, and I'm still here still here with my
rhinestone brimmed Stetson and new dress shirt

the country cowboy gentleman standing in the corner
counts sheep, it's all a quiet milling, and we're all wearing
masks because it is still the pandemic and we shouldn't
sit too close and there is no discussion of wars or
pestilence or climate change because we're dealing
with drooping lids and floating retinas and other
things that cause us pain even when in our best
dressed selves and we're feeling each others pain
because it may be about to worsen when the nurse
comes through the door and asks us to come in.
So we're sitting there and sure enough she come out
again for me and I pass by all those fantastic people I
have come to almost love and they sit there drawn
into themselves not saying anything, and that's okay
because I hear the music of their being there as we're
all leaning on each other in our way in the waiting
room. She takes me into a sterile operating room and
says there's a small tumor on your eyelid and this is
going to hurt, I can't lie, and presses a needle filled
with anesthetic into the skin below my eye, and as I
curl in pain adds and we'll get those cataracts out too.
It's going to hurt, I can't lie, but we'll change the way
you see.

Watching a Downy Woodpecker

I'm watching a downy woodpecker
silhouetted against storm clouds on
the highest branch of an ancient sycamore
tilting to the wind, sharpening beak
against fluid bark and pausing, then
picking what it finds into its mouth
jostling its feathers as the clouds
themselves are jostled against cloud.
What does it hope to find so far above
the ground where beetles burrow freely?
Perhaps one or two tired stringy grubs
within a stalk too thin to hold them
yet hanging on, they too small and cold.

I must go on and like that tuft of feather
tend to the little things I cannot catch
or keep for any length of time. The
messages of lovers, family, friends
that tie me to the world I love. I look
at my investments in the future, my
meager means of tying thoughts to
whatever it is that meets us at this time.

This is my job; Making skin tight marks
on paper as my sister falls dead across
the country where she sifted tax returns
and handed out the government doles
to those who could no longer work
one Administration to the next and next
a long gray highway of U.S. dreamers.
It is too cold to walk the fields today,
the winds too turbulent and I too small
and dark, too feebly feathered to fly
holding only what I can.

Waggle Dancing Amidst the Hive

Nothing smooth or graceful
in the frenetic sweep of my translucent wings;
no, they are more the frantic torment
of one small soul with a world to achieve.
These wings, weathervanes of life,
are pulsing with the energy of a song that is
transforming, planting, pollinating the universe.

'tho only a bee, I sing a universe of multitudes
captured in the cells of my compound eyes,
seeing every angle, every twist and fold
every fractal of each flower on the mountainside,
swarming among them dancing in ultraviolet
burrowing into the hearts of asters and milkweed,
drinking and eating their nectar and pollen
and dusting it to the evening stars.

My vision is immense, my three ocelli
adding to my compound eyes their shadings of the
heavens and the rolling clouds above me giving
depth, for an infinitely small insect upon the skin
of the universe yet demented with the dream of

implanting it all with life, with flowers that bloom
across an immense meadow with no end, and filling
each grain of earth with seeds to grow and feed the
song that now surrounds us.

I contain multitudes. My sense of smell so refined
I can smell tumors, disease, and the sickness of humans
wherever it occurs within their bodies, or zero in
on wild rose, spirea, Russian sage. I look forward over
the meadows and among the trees
        the towering maples, redbuds, weeping cherries.
and overhead into the shadows and light above us, the
clouds. I navigate by the sun, by the polarization of patterns
        of the sky, and by the Earth's magnetism,
and I am one with it all; these wings so small, so fragile
and luminous, they fill the world with life and song.

Within the Shadows of Invisible

There are no deer in the side yard this morning,
stepping out from the tall winter grasses
on silent feet, nibbling the buds from groundcover,
looking toward our window ears raised quizzically,
knowing we are here but not why or what we are
sensing danger in the midst of our kindness, fading
back into the landscape from which they come.

This is a wide, deep forest where the trees grow close,
so squeezed together they shiver in winter's wind
rather than standing tall and strong against it
their trunks and branches rubbing against each other,
hands and eyes tangled against the clouds.

This is a forest filled with invisible animals
that take their meals from the sun and shadow
and go uncounted about their time among us.
This is the forest unkempt, unlogged, pressing
against the cities undrawn by architects, un
lived in within the shadows of invisible.

Taking War as a Lesson in Humanity

The touch on a child's cheek
nothing at first, a butterfly in the tropics
heralding a coming typhoon, yet
lovely as one tiny breath of magic
too soon discarded in the collective mind
and manipulation of bonds and futures.

But for that child the touch remains
in the building of homes, the growing of grains,
the sloughing off of youth, hardening of hands,
copulations beneath a star tossed cosmos,
one set of genes into another, one life lost
almost meaningless outside the family
except for the touch that hand holds out.

Does a man make a difference?

The Shoebox at the End of the Universe

A light is leaking out of the shoebox at the end
of the universe and filtering down a long tunnel
of time. I am as empty as a cello holding my strings.
What has happened to all the girls I knew
beneath a midnight sky with the snow falling?
Where have our footsteps led us?

The shoebox holds a collection of small things
left over and tucked away behind an old man's
coats, some of them the brightness of a full moon,
others the oily writhing of nightcrawlers on a hook,
still others merely odors stagnant in an airless
space, or shapes no longer visible shifting without
    mass.

These are the creatures and creations, the lures
that pull at the fabric of improbability we live in.
They are the ghosts that have served as our guides
with words the texture of mildewed cardboard.

*

Mr. Tempis listens to the shambling steps drag up
the stairs of his tenement, the fumbling at his door.

Are you there, Marie? he calls out. Come in! Come in!
He turns the kettle on, lights a smoke, pulls out a chair
and nods his head as rats crawl up and down his walls.

He opens a drawer and touches flesh no longer there.
Mary Ann swirls about him, and Kelly, Paula, Genevieve,
names that no longer have substance to place them on
tumbled among sunsets, beaches on oceans and mountains,
worn down from the fractals of stone lost to time.

But I know them all, he says to the darkness and they all
listen to his words, heard above the taxicabs and ubers,
and there is a light coming from the crumpled shoebox,
if only a light could look out upon itself from its source.

Beagles Have Two Eyes

When Darwin sailed
all the men on board had two eyes
all the fish in the sea had two eyes
and all the gulls turning above had two
and the lice that lived upon the men each had two
and all the finches on the islands they came to
each had two like every other living thing,
and the islands had no eyes and so were not alive,
but every other living thing regardless of wing
or length of beak or length of inch per finch
had eyes on each side of the head
and a long and narrow digestive tract.

In not seeing this, our perception lacks

Jared Smith's poetry has appeared in hundreds of journals and anthologies in this country, Canada, Mexico, the U.K., and China. He has served on the Editorial Boards of *Home Planet News; The New York Quarterly; The Pedestal Magazine;* and *Turtle Island Quarterly,* as well as on the Boards of literary and arts non-profits in New York, Illinois, and Colorado. He is listed in *The Colorado Encyclopedia; Poets & Writers; Colorado Poets Center; Who's Who in America;* and other reference sources. He holds a Master's degree in Literature from New York University, and studied under The Great Books Program at St. John's College. He has taught at New York University and LaGuardia Community College (CCNY,) and worked as Director of Research and Education at an international laboratory, as Special Advisor to Argonne National Laboratory, and as an advisor to several White House Commissions under President William Clinton. He lives in Ellicott City, Maryland.

This project was made possible, in part, by generous support from the Osage Arts Community.

Osage Arts Community provides temporary time, space and support for the creation of new artistic works in a retreat format, serving creative people of all kinds — visual artists, composers, poets, fiction and nonfiction writers. Located on a 152-acre farm in an isolated rural mountainside setting in Central Missouri and bordered by ¾ of a mile of the Gasconade River, OAC provides residencies to those working alone, as well as welcoming collaborative teams, offering living space and workspace in a country environment to emerging and mid-career artists. For more information, visit us at www.osageac.org

Osage Arts Community

www.ingramcontent.com/pod-product-compliance
Lightning Source LLC
Chambersburg PA
CBHW030222140626
46545CB00012B/2853